The Lord's prayer is often one of the first prayers that young children learn. It is a difficult prayer for them to understand and rather than try to explain its meaning this book aims to help children towards their own appreciation of the Lord's prayer.

Each section of the book contains simple prayers and verses related to the Lord's prayer and relevant to the children's own experiences.
An alternative version of the Lord's prayer, used by many churches today, is given at the back of the book.

Acknowledgments
The compiler and publisher would like to thank the following for material included in this book: page 38 *God made the shore* by Amy Carmichael printed by kind permission of The Dohnavur Fellowship Corp. Ltd; page 13 *Moon come out* by Eleanor Farjeon from *Silver, Sand and Snow* published by Michael Joseph and used with permission; page 28 *Thank You for the world so sweet* by Edith Rutter Leatham printed by kind permission of Mrs Lorna Hill; page 26 *When I wake up in the morning* from *Infant Prayer* by Margaret Kitson and page 24 *God has given us work to do* from *Infant Praise* by Margaret Kitson both by kind permission of Oxford University Press; page 39 *Thank You, God, for stars in space* based on a poem by Lucile S. Reed and taken from *Sing for Joy* compiled and edited by Norman and Margaret Mealy © 1961 by The Seabury Press Inc and used with permission; page 9 *And God said the sun should shine* from *Come and Sing* published by Scripture Union; page 12 *Loving Father of all Children* from *The Nursery Song and Picture Book* by Winifred E. Barnard published by Arnold-Wheaton; and page 7 *I'm very glad of God* appears by kind permission of Alice Pullen. The publishers have made every effort to contact copyright holders and acknowledge sources of material in this book. Any omissions are unintentional and will be amended at the earliest opportunity.

First Edition

© LADYBIRD BOOKS LTD MCMLXXXIV

The Lord's Prayer

compiled by *HY MURDOCK*
illustrated by *MARTIN AITCHISON*

Ladybird Books Loughborough

The Lord's Prayer

Our Father, who art in heaven,
hallowed be thy name.
Thy kingdom come,
thy will be done
on earth as it is in heaven.
Give us this day our daily bread
and forgive us our trespasses,
as we forgive those that trespass
                        against us.
And lead us not into temptation
but deliver us from evil,
for thine is the kingdom, the power
and the glory, for ever and ever.
                        Amen

Our Father, who art in heaven, hallowed be thy name.

Dear God,
We put our hands together
and come to talk to You
by saying a prayer.

Help us to be quiet and still
so that we can come close to You
each time we pray.

Amen

I'm very glad of God:
His love takes care of me,
In every lovely thing I see
God smiles at me!

I'm very glad of God:
His love takes care of me,
In every lovely sound I hear
God speaks to me!

Alice Muriel Pullen

Thy kingdom come, thy will be done on earth as it is in heaven.

And God said the sun should shine;
The rain should fall;
  the flowers should grow.
And God said the birds should sing;
And it was so.
And God said the grass
      should grow;
  the trees bear fruit;
  the wind should blow.
And God said the stream
      should flow;
And it was so.

Teach us to love the world.
Help us to look after
all the beautiful things
You have given to us:
the trees and the flowers,
the birds and the animals.
Help us to be gentle
with small creatures:
ladybirds, beetles and butterflies;
and to look at delicate spiders' webs
without spoiling them.
Please help us to see all
the wonderful things in the world.

Amen

Hurt no living thing:
Ladybird, nor butterfly,
Nor moth with dusty wing,
Nor cricket chirping cheerily,
Nor grasshopper so light of leap,
Nor dancing gnat, nor beetle fat,
Nor harmless worms that creep.

Christina Rossetti

Thank You for night time
when I can rest.
For the moon which gives soft light
at night and the stars that twinkle
in the sky.
For my nice warm bed and the quiet
of the night — thank You, God.

Loving Father of all children,
I belong to Thee.
Through the daytime,
Through the night time,
Please take care of me.

Amen

Moon come out
And Sun go in,
Here's a soft blanket
To cuddle your chin.

Moon go in
And Sun come out,
Throw off your blanket
and bustle about.

Eleanor Farjeon

13

Dear God,
Thank You for caring for us.
Thank You for our mothers
and fathers,
Our brothers and sisters and
all our friends.
Please take care of my family
and friends always.

Amen

Dear God,
Please take care of all the people
  in the world.
Help me to remember those people
  who are not as lucky as I am:
those with no homes and no food;
those who are ill or unhappy.
Please take care of them.

Amen

Thank You, God, for clever people;
Those who have good ideas.
Help them to use their ideas
    to make the world a safer
    and happier place.

Amen

Take care of all the different
people of the world, with different
ways and different languages.
Help us to understand
and love them.

Amen

Thank You for babies
who are so wonderfully made:
For their tiny hands and feet,
their tiny nails, their soft skin
and warm smell.
Help us to be very gentle with them.

Amen

Dear God,
Please help old people,
    especially those who are lonely
    and have no one to visit them.
Take care of those who are ill.
Let us remember them
    and help them if we can.

                                    Amen

Dear Father God,
We thank You that we are able to see;
please help the blind who cannot see.
We thank You that we are able to hear;
please help the deaf who cannot hear.
We thank You that we are able
    to speak;
please help the dumb
    who cannot speak...

We thank You that we can run
and jump and play.
Please help sick and crippled
children everywhere.

Amen

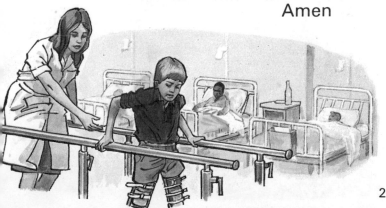

O God, thank You for all we do
  at school:
for the pictures we paint,
for the models we make,
for the games we play,
the songs we sing,
the work we do.
Thank You for our teachers and friends
and for happy times at school.

                        Amen

Thank You for happy times at home:
For times when we enjoy
playing with our friends;
for birthdays
and for special times
when we have surprises.
Help us to make others happy too.

Amen

God has given us work to do,
Work to do for Him.
God has given us friends to help,
Friends to help for Him.
We will work for God today,
We will help our friends.
We shall be so glad today,
Glad to work for Him.

Margaret Kitson

Dear God,
Help me to learn all I can and to
  understand the world around me;
to try hard and to do my
  best work always.

Amen

When I wake up in the morning
Thank You, God, for being there.
When I go to school each day
Thank You, God, for being there.
When I'm playing with my friends
Thank You, God, for being there.
And when I go to bed at night
Thank You, God, for being there.

Amen

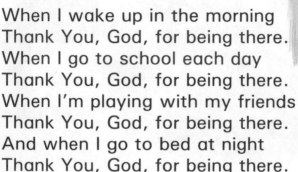

New things to do,
New places to go,
New things to learn,
New people to know,
New songs to sing,
New games to play,
We'll try not to spoil
This happy new day.

Amen

Give us this day our daily bread

Thank You for the world so sweet,
Thank You for the food we eat,
Thank You for the birds that sing,
Thank You God for everything.

Edith Rutter Leatham

Dear God,
Help me to remember all the people
who work to give us food:
farmers working on the land;
fishermen at sea;
and people who work
in factories and shops.
Thank You for looking after them.

Amen

For seeds to plant in the ground,
For rain that makes them grow,
For sun that ripens the crops
And the people who gather the
harvest for our food,
Father, we thank You.

Amen

Dear Lord,
Please help those who are hungry
and do not have enough food to eat.
Help me to remember them
when I am hungry
and wanting something to eat,
and when I am greedy
and asking for too much.

Amen

Forgive us our trespasses, as we forgive those that trespass against us. And lead us not into temptation

Dear God,
I am sorry for the things that
    I have done wrong:
for bad temper and angry words,
for being greedy and not sharing,
for making other people unhappy.
Please help me to think of others.

Amen

Dear God,
I often see my best friends
with things that I would like;
Some money or some chocolate,
or even a new bike.
I know it's wrong to want things.
I know they are not free.
Please help me, God, to be quite
strong about these things I see
And never harm or take things
which don't belong to me.

Amen

Dear God,
Help us always to tell the truth
 even when we have done wrong.
Please help us to be kind and helpful
 to everyone we meet.
Help us to share
 and to think of others,
Now and always.

                    Amen

Dear God,

Please help me to be kind
to all animals.

Help me to take care of my pets and
to make sure they always have
food and water.

I will play with them and stroke
them gently.

Please help me not to be rough or
unkind to any of Your creatures.

Amen

Deliver us from evil,

Dear God,
Please take care of me
  when I feel afraid:
When it is dark and I am alone,
When I have done wrong
  and I need to say I'm sorry,
When I am frightened,
  because I have a pain.
Thank You, Lord.

Amen

*Be near me, Lord Jesus,
I ask you to stay
Close by me for ever
and love me, I pray.*

Amen

Dear Father,
Please take care of
all the children in the world.
Keep them safe from danger,
now and always.

Amen

For thine is the kingdom, the power and the glory,

God made the shore,
 rocks and sand and sea,
Little, lovely shells –
He made me.
God feeds the fish
 swimming in the sea,
Feeds them every day –
He feeds me.
God's behind the storm
 lashing up the sea.
God's within the calm –
He loves me.

Amy Carmichael

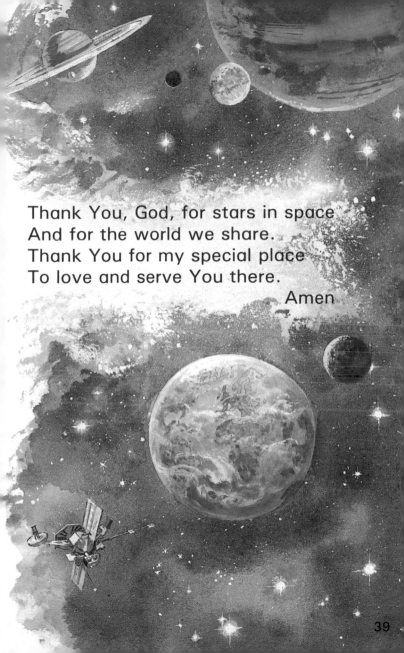

Thank You, God, for stars in space
And for the world we share.
Thank You for my special place
To love and serve You there.

Amen

Dear Lord,
When I see huge mountains
and tall trees;
When I hear rumbling thunder,
the roaring wind and
the crashing of the sea on rocks,
I feel very small but I know that
You are taking care of me.

Amen

For the golden sunshine,
the twinkling stars and
the gentle light of the moon,
We thank You, God.

For the velvety sky at night,
the blue summer sky and the
fluffy white clouds,
We thank You, God.

Amen

For ever and
ever.

AMEN

Help us to do the things we should,
To be to others kind and good
In all we do, in all we say,
To grow more loving every day.

Help us to remember
All Your love and care,
Trust in You and love You
Always, everywhere.
                    Amen

Some people say this version of

The Lord's Prayer

Our Father in heaven,
hallowed be Your name,
Your kingdom come,
Your will be done,
on earth as in heaven.
Give us today our daily bread.
Forgive us our sins
as we forgive those
who sin against us.
Do not bring us to the time of trial
but deliver us from evil.
For the kingdom, the power
and the glory are Yours
now and forever.

Amen